PRACTICES

PRACTICES
MORNING AND EVENING
~ helping moms have happier homes ~

KERI MAE LAMAR

A Happy Home Media
KINGSTON, WASHINGTON

Copyright © 2018 by Keri Mae Lamar.

All rights reserved. No part of this publication may be reproduced, distributed or transmitted in any form or by any means, including photocopying, recording, or other electronic or mechanical methods, without the prior written permission of the publisher, except in the case of brief quotations embodied in critical reviews and certain other noncommercial uses permitted by copyright law. For permission requests, write to the publisher, addressed "Attention: Permissions Coordinator", at the address below.

Keri Mae Lamar/AHappyHomeMedia.com
P.O. Box 1304
Kingston, WA 98346

Author photograph: Logan Lamar

Links referenced or recommended in this book may be affiliate links, to which the author earns a small commission.

Scripture taken from the authorized King James version.

Practices/Keri Mae Lamar – 1st. ed.
ISBN 978-0-9961100-2-0

10   9   8   7   6   5   4   3   2

To my family,
who allow me the time and freedom
to pursue PRACTICES
that not only enrich my own life,
but in turn, enrich theirs.

First, live for God one day at a time. Whatever long-term plans we may have, we need to get into the habit of planning each day's business in advance, either first thing each morning or (better, I think) the day before. Glorifying God should be our constant goal, and to that end we need to acquire the further habit of reviewing before God as each day closes how far we have done as we planned, or whether and why and how far we changed the plan to fit new circumstances and fresh insights, and in any case how far we did the best we could for our God, and how far we fell short of doing that.

–J.I. Packer, *Finishing Our Course with Joy,*
as quoted by John Piper

Contents

Introduction xiii

1. First Things First 1
   Tyrant Number One
   Tyrant Number Two

2. Morning Practices 7
   Awaken
   Study
   Write
   Bathe
   Make
   Nourish
   Move
   Learn
   Look
   Plan
   Smile

3. Evening Practices 33
   Clear the Sink
   Babies to Bed
   Look
   Plan
   Create
   Read
   Connect
   Pray

4. Implement 59
    Keep the Main Thing the Main Thing
    Seasons
    Christian Liberty
    60 Day Calendar
    In Closing

Resources 67
    Some Good Reads
    Journal Prompts
    Other Mama Practices
    60 Day Calendar
    Links
    Next Steps

My PRACTICES 107
    Morning
    Evening
    Seasonal

Other Books by Keri Mae 113

INTRODUCTION

But this I say, brethren, the time is short...
– 1 Corinthians 7:29
The days are long, but the years are short.
– anonymous

YOU KNOW THIS, already, don't you. That's why we as mothers try to fit in as much as we can into every day, from homekeeping to homeschooling to side jobs or businesses, driving so many places for so many hours, grabbing the clock by the ticker and making it scream to give up the additional minutes we demand. That's why on a Saturday morning our eyes open and in the initial fog we might think, "Weekend already..." but BAM! the list of things We-Must-Accomplish-Before-

Monday light up like a Vegas skyline across our minds and off we go.

And it's not that we don't want to relax and enjoy our lives. It's simply that everything around us screams in terrible urgency. The baby is crying. The toddler is hungry. The fridge needs a grocery trip. Appointments need to be made and kept, and the homework between is daunting and perhaps a bit uninspiring at best.

Meanwhile, in the waiting times (and they are there: in waiting chairs, waiting for the pot to boil, waiting for the baby to get into stage 4 sleep while rocking, rocking, rocking...) we ride the scroll. Our eyes flip flip flip like hovering hummingbirds through our social media accounts, noting who is doing what and when and why can't that be me right now. Our forefinger pauses when a photo catches our breath because it pings a memory in our heart or a desire in our soul. That house. That craft. That place. Those sweet children. Behind the glass, and yet close enough to exude a transcendent scent.

What is needed is not for the circumstances to change, for your children to hurry up and grow and

PRACTICES

be gone. For if you mother with that sort of urgency, your lament will be real and raw when tomorrow they fly, for tomorrow they shall. Rather, what's needed is an incorporation of PRACTICES to slow the pace and yet allow you to get more done. Where undone chores may chide you from every corner, but you have a righteous and peaceable response to them. Where your dreams, the ones you had when you were nine, still not only have a place in your life, but a real plan and current pleasure.

It's not only possible to be present today in all of your life, it's desperately needed. Ongoing stress feeds unhealthy habits and, unfortunately, those habits lead to poor choices, which feeds ongoing stress. That's why we're tired, unhealthy, financially struggling, and losing relationship with our family members. That's also why we scroll so much.

If you want to start your day with hope and end your day with satisfaction, you must be willing to address your current PRACTICES and strive to make them better. I say "strive" because change is not easy. It takes courage and quite a bit of stubbornness, and fear or anger will seek to derail you.

The PRACTICES I share with you have been helpful to me for decades. They are not complicated and you might argue I am saying nothing new. But they are costly. You will need to lay down your avoidance and your argumentation and simply do them. For how long? For as long as you desire to enjoy the days as you are in them, whatever the circumstances.

I pray this will be as helpful to you as it has been to me.

CHAPTER ONE

First Things First

Whatever good things we build end up building us.

– Jim Rohn

YOU MAY BE EAGER TO BEGIN, but I am compelled to warn you ahead of time of a couple of "tyrants" that will get in the way. Recognizing these tyrants will better equip you to be successful in making those small changes that will give you beautiful returns.

TYRANT NUMBER ONE

Screen time
Perhaps you are one of few who would be most sincerely surprised, but screen time has robbed

mothers – with their permission and access – of time, energy, peace, and contentment. Perhaps you are also one of many who are assured of their own moderation and balance, complete control of its pernicious tentacles. If so, *yay!* But may I encourage you to test this objectively, to completely reassure yourself you are indeed master of this tyrant?

The simplest way to do so is to download the *Moment* app.[1] It keeps track of time spent on your smartphone and reports your activity back to you. Try it for a week. If you feel the report from your phone is reasonable – and you are making good progress on your other goals, and your relationships are edifying – then cheers. If, however, you are introduced to the ugly reality you've been badly bitten by the addictive snake of distraction, rejoice! You have met your first tyrant, and it is unmasked.

Thankfully, it can be tamed. You don't have to put it to death (although, yes, you can). The *Moment* app can help you to set time limits, including which apps you are allowing unclocked. You may also set screen-free times. Your phone will either start yelling at you to get off at the specified time or – for those needing it – will force quit on its own.

Furthermore, I strongly encourage you to do a media fast on a regular basis. This can be as simple as an hour a day, a weekend every season, or a week every year. Insidiously, screen time has too often become synonymous with breathing, and unless the air is thinned, not many recognize their slavish state to this technology. Personally, unless I am aware of an ongoing emergency (such as a friend having a baby at any time), my phone is turned off a couple of hours before bed, and stays off for at least an hour after waking. That alone has helped me tremendously in my PRACTICES.

TYRANT NUMBER TWO

Shackles

If you have repented and put your trust in Jesus Christ, then God has redeemed you from the shackles of sin and given to you Christian liberty. This means unlike joining a local church or practicing the sacraments, Christians are free to live within the bounds of their own consciences as they understand Scripture dictates.

In other words, tools such as those I am giving you are simply that: tools. They are not masters over you. The point of these PRACTICES is not for you to serve THEM, but for them to serve YOU. They are not meant to be perfected; they are meant to equip you to cultivate the kind of life and living your spirit longs for, to the best you can, on this fallen world surrounded by sinful people (including the one in the mirror).

Understanding this, you are less likely to read these PRACTICES and immediately object, "I can't....!" Saying "I can't" is self-defeating and arises because of assumptions made which may or may not be true. How do you *know* a particular PRACTICE would be hard/boring/dumb/worthless?

Maybe you've "tried it before". Perhaps. But that seems akin to saying food makes you ill, when in reality it was the greasy, fried dinner that made you sick and not "food" itself. Learn from what derailed you before and grow from there. Did you try journaling years ago, and it flopped? Question why. Did you have your smartphone on at the time? Did you even like the pen and paper you were using? Did

PRACTICES

you give up because you had nothing to say, instead of looking for good prompts to answer?

You will not do any of these perfectly, so let go of thinking these PRACTICES are in and of themselves meant to get you to *Pleasantville*. Rather, they are helpful tools to engage you in your life, and are supposed to be pleasurable in and of themselves. Do them for the pleasure it gives you, in real time. Replace "I can't..." with *"How* can I..." and start thinking (and seeing) differently.

Ready?

In order to end up in a place you desire more, you need to change direction. Thankfully, that doesn't have to be a massive undertaking. A few cranks of the wheel, little by little, still delivers you to a massively different locale at the end of the journey, even if your PRACTICES are not practiced daily.

So set your sights on your destination, and let's get started.

Chapter Two

Morning Practices

*Relying on God has to start all over everyday,
as if nothing has yet been done.*

– C.S. Lewis

AWAKEN

WAKE UP BEFORE YOUR BABIES DO.

I know. You're tired. You were probably up multiple times during the night. Even so, rise up before your babies do.

An alarm clock probably isn't necessary. When your eyes flutter and recognize morning, it is time to get up. If you hear your babies stirring, it is *especially* time to get up. Getting physically out of bed will help you to get a great start on your day. Otherwise, you begin the day already behind, and it is very difficult to catch up.

If you are simply too exhausted to do this, consider:

- Are you staying up too late? If hours were worth points, consider the hours you sleep before midnight worth *double* the hours you get after midnight. Chances are, your babies were sleeping for many hours before you went to bed.

- Are you sleeping with your smartphone nearby? Between the radiation, the light, and any notifications, this little device could be playing havoc on the quality of rest you are getting. We keep all electronics out of the bedroom, turn off our router at night, and make our rooms as dark as possible.

PRACTICES

- Is your bed a luxurious nest? Because we spend a third of our lives sleeping, the quality and comfort of the mattress is extremely important for deep rest. This doesn't have to be an expensive endeavor. We bought our chemical free 12" mattress from Amazon[2] and it has been wonderful.

- When you are able, buy the best pillows and linens you can afford. For our 25th anniversary, I bought my long-awaited linen sheets and feather pillows. After sleeping on them, I cannot believe I waited so long to do so. They are a dream.

- Is your body trying to digest a heavy meal, drugs, or late-night alcohol? Your body is wonderfully designed to heal, restore, and replenish during sleep, but if there is too much food or whatnot in the system, it will put off restoration until digestion is accomplished. Priorities, you know. Also, if you are on medication of any kind, do diligent research to see if sleeplessness is a side effect.[3]

- If insomnia is a problem, I urge you to seek a solution. Many people around the world have been helped with herbs, homeopathy[4] and Biblical counseling.[5]

If you are up and out of bed before your babies are, rejoice! You have a beautiful, quiet start to your day and can embark on even more Morning PRACTICES should you choose.

If, *whoops, too late*...all is not lost! Try to grab the quickest shower you can, get dressed, and brush your teeth and hair. You can do it all in less than 10 minutes, and you'll be glad you did when UPS shows up with a package or a neighbor comes knocking for a question.

After AWAKEN, the most important PRACTICES are going to be NOURISH, LOOK and PLAN. So, skip down to those until you have quiet time later in the day (say, nap or quiet times for the children). Then, you can backup to do one or more of what you missed that morning, especially STUDY time.

STUDY

My voice shalt thou hear in the morning, O LORD; in the morning will I direct my prayer unto thee, and will look up.

– Psalms 5:3

When my conversion occurred, I had a real hunger for the Word of God. I could not get enough of reading my Bible. I was as a woman completely parched who had discovered living water and I drank and drank it all in. As I had no idea where to start, I began in the Proverbs, because I liked to collect "quotes", and Proverbs was full of them.

Since then, I have kept a daily PRACTICE of Bible reading. Some seasons are as if I am living on scraps, especially when ill, postpartum, or dealing with the fatigue that occurs in rare chaotic times such as moving. In other seasons, I have the luxury of an hour or more to read, take notes, read concordances and dictionaries, and study maps. Whether it is a short dip or a long leisurely swim, I urge you to make daily reading a priority. It is as necessary as your daily food:

> *Thy words were found, and I did eat them; and thy word was unto me the joy and rejoicing of mine heart: for I am called by thy name, O LORD God of hosts.*
>
> – Jeremiah 15:16

> *...I have esteemed the words of his mouth more than my necessary food.*
>
> – Job 23:12b

Perhaps you feel this is not necessary, and I may be trampling upon grace and Christian liberty. If so, I wonder why you would want to shy from hearing from the Lord, whom you claim to love. For whom else do you claim to love, and yet avoid or neglect?

> *How shall we escape, if we neglect so great salvation; which at the first began to be spoken by the Lord, and was confirmed unto us by them that heard him....*
>
> – Hebrews 2:3

My sisters, do not neglect this. Do not think reading devotionals, Christian books or blogs, or even listening to sermons online, are a substitute. Those things may or may not be profitable. But reading the Word of God is always profitable, even if you do not feel so at the time.

There are many ways to incorporate Scripture reading into the day, but I find the morning reading most edifying. My mind is fresh and, as I have not turned on my smartphone or needed to tend to a child, there isn't else to distract me. I don't like to let my eyes read anything else before I get to the Bible, so if I am having a late morning, so be it. The newspaper, magazines, and any homework must wait until I read the Word.

Below are many ways I have used to keep my reading habit. Choose one, and begin today.

- Read the Proverbs, matching the chapter to the day of the month. If it is the 15th, for example, read Proverbs chapter 15, and so forth.

- Read the Psalms, beginning with matching the chapter to the day of the month, and then adding 30, to the end of the book. If it is the 15th, again for example, read Psalms 15, 45, 75, 105, and 135.

- Read straight through the Bible, beginning in Genesis, including the seemingly boring genealogies and chronologies (pray for the Lord to teach you through them!), all the way through Revelation. Then, start again at the beginning. It is so fascinating to find Jesus in every single book of the Bible. If you are able, reading three to four chapters per day will get you through the Bible in a year.

- When you come to a verse that gives you pause, PAUSE. Think about it. Pray for God to teach you. Is it convicting? Repent. Does it remind you of someone? Pray. Are you confused by it? Stop and look up the passage or word in a commentary, or do a word study.

- To do a word study, write the verse out onto a sheet of paper. Look up what seem to be key words in the dictionary. I especially appreciate the *Webster's 1828*.[6] Then, look up those words in a concordance. I use the King James Bible and find KJVbible.net[7] an excellent (and undistractible) search engine. Copy and paste the verses onto a document, print, and then cut them out. Then, group the verses into common themes or definitions. I find this to be an excellent study and learn a lot.

- If reading is absolutely not an option, due to eye constraints or fatigue, then *listen*[8] to the Bible instead. You can make this app not count for your screen time if you have the *Moment* app,[1] and still nurse and rock the baby with both hands while drinking in the Word of God.

- In seasons when you are afforded more time, study deeply. The best Bible study I am aware of is Precept.org,[9] and I long to do it more.

- Memorize scripture, so it is with you always. I like to write out verses onto index cards and tape them where I regularly am. For accountability and great PRACTICE tools (including an app), I use and recommend ScriptureMemory.com.[10] It is an excellent program, even for children, and I have found it to bear much (and sustainable) fruit.

Lastly, BEWARE of Bible studies and devotionals which focus on emotionalism and on what the passage *feels* like or means "to you". Unfortunately, I find many of these targeted (and quite successfully so) towards women. The Bible isn't about YOU or ME. It's about JESUS. At the end of your reading and/or study, your heart ought to be praising God more.

WRITE

Other than studying the Bible, no other PRACTICE has helped my thinking more than keeping a journal. I've kept a journal since I was 13. A journal is simply a private place to write down anything going on in my mind. This includes plans, dreams, rants, prayers, poems, and answers to prompts from a variety of places. I write for about 10-15 minutes, more on a good day.

PRACTICES

There is brain research pointing to the real work handwriting does for mental health and processing information. If this interests you, I encourage you to seek and study it; it is fascinating. For the purpose of this book, however, simply know that taking a pen or pencil in your physical hand (versus typing onto a keyboard) is beneficial.

Writing helps you process all of the thoughts in your head. It helps you gain understanding, wisdom, and clarity. It helps you think through problems, and relieves stress. Writing is actually not only invented by, but important to God. Look up "write" in a concordance and read all of the commands to WRITE. If simply thinking upon or reminiscing over events was enough, we wouldn't need to put our pens to paper.

However, what helps me to look forward to writing is not the understanding of how good it is for me or how much my mind profits. I know these things, but knowledge does not lead me to an eager session of writing, no matter how satisfied I am when I am finished.

What gives me pleasure in writing are two things:

1) Having a notebook and pen I like. Doesn't that sound silly? But that is what woos me. I love the tactile feel of the paper, and how the pen glides effortlessly across the page. It makes handwriting easier and less like pushing. If you are not enjoying your journal or notebook, you won't look forward to using it. My favorite place to look for notebooks and pens is at Jet Pens.[11] Yes, I might spend a little more for my paper, but in the grand scheme of things, it is less expensive than therapy and has less side effects than caffeine or drugs for my mental health. My favorite everyday pen is Pilot's Premium Gel Roller G2, in a fine 0.7mm tip.[12] I encourage you most wholeheartedly to find paper and pen (or pencil) you really love.

2) Having prompts to answer. Many times, I want to write, but my mind feels blank. Now I *know* it's NOT blank – it's too full of too many emotions, too many thoughts

PRACTICES

– but at times I have trouble simply knowing where to start or what to write about. I appreciate having prompts because I can quickly get to writing and spend less time pondering about a subject (as time ticks by and my morning slips away). You can find prompts in many places. Try your library for a book on keeping a journal or diary. Also, as a bonus (*yay!*), I am including 60 days of prompts for you to consider. They are at the back of this book in the Resources. And don't worry if it takes you 80 or more days to do them.

You don't need to feel constrained by writing in and of itself. You could also try doodling and drawing pictures, or art journaling. The point is to have a place in which you physically do the work of not only thinking, but of transferring those thoughts into a safe place. Don't worry if you have nothing to say. Simply get into the habit of showing up, and the words will come.

What to do with finished journals? That is up to you. I saved mine for many years, thinking I would want them to revisit. But in the end, I decided it was best for me to destroy the books as I filled them. Thus, my thoughts are between myself and God, and I have no constraints or worries about who may come across them. After all, the work was (and is) in the DOING of it, not the HAVING DONE it.

Before I throw out a finished book, I take a highlighter pen in hand and read through my journal. I might find phrases or ideas I am still wanting to ponder and dig deeper into, or an idea I still want to do. I might find a recurring theme I did not see as I was writing but now needs further consideration. I find it a helpful PRACTICE to do this, as I do not want to forget my lessons learned or "aha" moments. Then, I transfer those thoughts or phrases or questions into my new notebook. And *those* make great prompts.

I've also ripped out pages which were meaningful for me to keep, and slipped them into other notebooks. Some pages I have torn into strips, and glued them into the background of my mixed media art, not wanting to part with good fruit my writing brought forth. As you can see, there are many options for a finished (or abandoned) notebook. Do with it what seems right for you, but do keep in mind other eyes may find your work. And those eyes are not the point of this writing exercise.

BATHE

Perhaps you are aghast I would include BATHE here. Of course! What an obvious thing, you may be thinking. However, I am not speaking of the quick pop in the shower. Unless you have any health problems exacerbated by bathing (ask your doctor), I am encouraging you to *soak*.

I hope you have access to a bathtub. Bathing in hot water does so much good. Not only does it cleanse the body of toxins, it relieves muscle tension, hydrates your skin, and encourages circulation. It's very calming to the nervous system, and cleanses the skin by opening pores. If you add epsom salts to the bath, you can reduce the harmful effects of radiation we are all bombarded by, plus get added magnesium for further wellbeing.

Taking a hot bath is wonderful at the end of the day, especially a couple of hours before bedtime, but I find I rarely give myself that luxury in the evening despite my best intentions. Sometimes, whatever happens during the day derails those plans. If I take a soaking bath every other day or so in the morning, I find it very helpful. Showering on the other days, of course, is necessary for cleanliness. Even here, however, you can make a pleasant experience. Clear out bottles and soaps you do not love and make room for those you do. Don't over-clean; when your skin is healthy, it is full of beneficial bacteria keeping that outer organ better protected against invaders. Areas really needing to be soaped up are the "pits and bits". Unless there is physical dirt, other areas aren't in as much need of soaping and thereby ridding all of those beneficial bugs living on us. And, no, you won't stink.

Here is my favorite recipe to make your bathing experience more delightful:

> In a stainless steel bowl, mix:
> - 2 cups epsom salts
> - 1/2 cup sea salt
> - 1 TB almond oil
> - 2 drops lavender essential oil
> - 2 drops bergamot essential oil
> - 2 drops grapefruit essential oil

In another bowl, mix 1 cup of dried herbs (I like dried roses, linden, and lavender...but you can try your own mix). Pour steaming hot water over it, and let it steep while you run the bath.

Then, strain the herbs and pour the salts mix into your tub and enjoy.

P.S. If you have chlorine in your house water, you can dechlorinate your bath with vitamin C tablets. That way, you don't have to soak in or breathe in any chlorine. We use Vitabath.[13]

P.P.S. You can take a soak and listen to your Bible at the same time.

MAKE

MAKE your bed. Throughout the day, you will probably see your bed multiple times. The whole house may be in complete disarray: toys on the floors, dishes piled up, children bouncing off the walls...but your bed will be a beacon of promise of relaxation to come. Making your bed also makes it easier to lie upon for a little rest or nap later on in the day (*highly* recommended if you are pregnant or have littles napping). If you find the task too much of a bother, consider your decor might be getting in the way. I know many pillows on a bed might look pretty, but if they are never off the floor, they are not doing much to bless your home. So MAKE your bed and have it look pretty and inviting for the evening to come, when your rest will be well deserved.

NOURISH

Well into adulthood, I began skipping breakfast on a regular basis. I was immediately busy with the day, and though I fed my babies a wholesome meal, I was happy with only a mug of hot tea and maybe a corner of toast as I was cleaning up. Besides, I wasn't hungry, so I certainly did not want to give my body food when it wasn't asking for it.

However.

As it turns out, I was getting more and more tired. Fatigued, even. I figured it was because of my aging, multiple pregnancies, interrupted sleep, and lack of exercise. Makes sense, doesn't it? So I got more rest. I signed up for 90 minute intense workout programs. And even though I continued aging (and having babies), I wasn't feeling better.

That's when I learned not having a growling tummy in the morning was actually not a good sign for me at all. My metabolism wasn't working well, and it was stressing my body, and that ongoing stress (along with, hello, over-exercising) was whacking my metabolism (see the cycle?). Skipping my morning meal also made it less likely I'd eat nourishing food later, because when "later" came around I was too hungry to care about proper preparation.

Healing began when I started making myself eat a little breakfast, especially with protein, and I continue this PRACTICE today. I don't use protein powders, however, because the manner in which they are processed is not good for my body. I usually eat eggs gathered by hens raised on green grass and bugs. My favorite meal is an omelette with leftover vegetables, sometimes with cheese, and always with a touch of real extra virgin olive oil.[14] Other mornings, I might eat leftover meat from the night before. I usually enjoy a latte or hot tea later in the morning while homeschooling. With regards to other drink, I will have 4-6oz of kefir smoothie on occasion, but otherwise strictly limit juices and smoothies because of the blood sugar rushes and strain on my pancreas.

Eating in the first hour or two of waking keeps my blood sugars controlled and my energy level throughout the day. This may or may not be true for your own body, but it is something to consider if you have been skipping breakfast and have other symptoms such as fatigue, stressed skin, thinning hair, mood swings, poor digestion, sleep disturbances, or subnormal body temperature.

The little book which helped me see this "aha" moment was *The Nourished Metabolism* by Elizabeth Walling.[15] It's a short read but has practical helps as well as directions on how to test your body temperature. I have a master's degree in Holistic Nutrition and am also a chapter leader for the Weston A. Price foundation, so nothing in the book was really new. But I appreciated how simple her writing and tips were, and I was encouraged by her tone.

PRACTICES

Here is a recipe for my favorite porridge, which I originally got from a Vitaclay recipe catalog. I enjoy this when I need a break from eggs, and I love a cup of it with plenty of butter. We like to let it soak overnight in the Vitaclay pot,[16] and set the timer for it to be finished in the morning. But you could totally make this the morning you need it – just make sure to allow enough time for it to cook.

> Mix into a pot, and cook on low for an hour:
> 1 cup steel cut oats
> 1/4 quinoa (rinsed)
> 1 TB chia seeds
> 6 cups milk
> 1/4 cup dried fruit
> vanilla or cinnamon powder as desired

Whenever and whatever you eat in the morning, make sure it is something NOURISHing. Treat your body like the temple it is, and it will better serve you.

MOVE

For some women, moving in the morning is best. Personally, I enjoy taking a daily walk in the afternoon, but I did not want to miss this as a Morning PRACTICE possibility for you. Some moms I know do stretching or other DVD-led exercise programs, and getting it out of the way before the other rigors of the day blesses them. My current favorite exercise program is Mutu System,[17] and I wish I had known about it even a decade ago. It is perfect for mothers of all ages, in all stages.

LEARN

It is prudent to learn something about what is going on in our culture, country, and world on a regular basis, so we may be informed and better able to engage. However, most mothers I know do not have time to read through newspapers on a daily basis. Furthermore, so much of what is relayed through mass media stimulates fear or offers countless visual portrayals of evil. We *know* there is evil in the world; we do not need to constantly feed ourselves reports of it. One of my current Morning PRACTICES is to fit

PRACTICES

in a listen of Albert Mohler's *The Briefing*[18] while I am getting ready for my day. I find the content beneficial and appreciate the Christian worldview.

LOOK

LOOK at your calendar. Is there an appointment scheduled today? Are there friends coming over? Is your rent due on Tuesday? LOOK at today and also the week ahead. That way, you will not be surprised or miss an appointment. You'll also know if it's a good day to (fill in the blank) when your kids ask if it's okay for them to (fill in the blank) or a friend texts you for a coffee date.

PLAN

In the same manner, LOOK at what you are PLANning to prepare, cook, and eat today. I find it stressful to approach suppertime and not have any idea of what I'm supposed to serve for the meal. That's the hour when I might be short with the children and ultimately serve something not very NOURISHing, not to mention more expensive.

NOURISHing foods take time and thought. A soup for supper takes a good broth, which begins about a day ahead of time. Likewise for sourdough bread, ferments, and marinated meats (did you know marinating your pork in an acidic bath is crucial for good blood health?[19]). Cutting up vegetables takes time. Preparing any sort of meat from the freezer takes time to thaw. Soaking beans takes time, not to mention cooking them.

Thoughtfully planning and preparing a nourishing meal for yourself and your family is one of the deepest ways I know to show love. It takes love to care enough to research what those foods ought to be, because in today's world we aren't taught by tradition and example anymore but by propaganda and politics. We simply do not have a society full of robust and vibrantly healthy people, so following in popular footsteps of fast food, processed grocery offerings, and too many restaurant meals, isn't going to change your family's health destination.

So PLAN what the meals are going to be today (and into tomorrow). Do you need to get the chicken out now to marinate for tonight? Did you think you were going to make sandwiches for lunch, but *whoops*...you're out of bread? Maybe you'll take those leftovers from last night and turn it all into a soup instead...*hmmm*...better get out the broth you froze last week so it will be ready for lunch....

If you know in advance what your PLAN is for the next several meals, you will have a better, happier day focusing your mind on other things because you LOOKed ahead and have your family's nourishment under your very wise and loving control. You and your family will be healthier for it, and you'll spend less time and energy caring for challenging illnesses that come along when meals are not thought out.

SMILE

I know. That's easy to do if you were able to do many of these PRACTICES. But what about those mornings when you get up late or are jolted out of bed by vomiting children? It happens. Do the best you can to get those things under control without panicking, and when you are ready, relax and smile. Let that smile stream out of your soul through your eyes. Try it, you'll like it. And so will your family. Don't let your circumstances dictate the quality of your smile.

Let your smile reflect that though you may not have everything together, you know the One who does, and because of that, it is all going to be okay. And, it is.

How long does all of this take? Well, if I'm blessed enough to have 60-90 minutes in the morning before my obligations start calling, I can do them all. Otherwise, 45 minutes to an hour is usually enough to fill my spiritual, mental, emotional, and physical needs in the morning and to give me a great start to my day.

Choose your own PRACTICES. Start with what you can, and remember: Perfectionism is a tyrant. Don't let it rule your efforts.

Have a happy morning!

Chapter Three

Evening Practices

*We didn't have television in those days,
and many people didn't even have radios.
My mother would read aloud
to my father and me in the evening.*
– Beverly Cleary

CLEAR THE SINK

NOTHING DRAINS MY ENERGY FASTER in the morning than coming down to the kitchen with a full and dirty sink waiting for me. The birds outside are chirping, the sun is streaming fresh light, the day is new with God's mercies...and I have to spend time and energy scraping dirty, smelly dishes. Not fun.

So it is my PRACTICE to have a clean kitchen., This is the list I go through each evening:

- ✓ sink cleared
- ✓ dishes done (including put away)
- ✓ counters wiped down
- ✓ floors swept
- ✓ trash and recycling out

It doesn't have to be a chore. In fact, it can be one of the most pleasant parts of the day.

And, if you've kept up on cleaning after every meal, it ought not be much of a burden.

Another way to have less to wash up is to make sure you are cleaning up as you prepare meals. In other words, while you are waiting for the water to boil, or the butter to melt, or the onions to fry...clear the sink, or put those mugs into the dishwasher, or wash the measuring cups you used, or wipe down the fridge from an earlier splat. Here a little, there a little, it gets done.

One thing I like to do is have a "Start-and-Stop" PRACTICE. In other words, for tasks I find hard to get going on (such as a dirty kitchen), I come up with a Start-and-Stop PRACTICE. My favorite kitchen Start-and-Stop PRACTICE is to light a candle by the sink (start) and then blow it out when all is finished (stop). Other people in my family like to listen to podcasts, music, or even the ball game.

Another idea is to use products you love.

My favorite soap for dishwashing is Mrs. Meyer's Dish Soap.[20] The Iowa Pine is scent is my very favorite for the winter season.

My favorite countertop cleaner is Zum Clean.[21] I like all the scents, but my absolute favorite is Sea Salt. *Gah*...makes me feel like I'm at a summer beach cabin rather than the middle of suburbia.

These cleaning brands are pricier than most, but they not only make cleaning a more pleasant experience, they are also concentrated, so a little bit goes a long way. I find these brands simply last longer than the cheaper ones in our own household. Your mileage may vary.

It is definitely worth the money to purchase cleaning supplies that are not only better for septic systems (or the environment, in general), but also for your hands and nose. Definitely seek out products you look forward to using. And then, use them with pleasure.

BABIES TO BED

Yes, put your babies to bed. Make a predictable and fun routine, and stick to it, so your babies will feel secure and safe. When my babies were young, Daddy bathed them while I cleaned the kitchen, so we could spend time with one another afterwards without doing chores. That's not to say "I wash, you dry" isn't quality time together, but it's nice when you can be together without having to do housework.

Children need not only quality sleep, but quantity sleep, like twelve hours overnight. This means, if you wake at 6:00AM and they bed down the night before at 8:00PM, you'll have a good two hours before they're up to do your Morning PRACTICES. This is provided you make your bedtime 10:00PM. With this schedule, not only will you get a good eight hours of rest, but – if you're doing your math – you'll have two hours in the evening to do your Evening PRACTICES, too. Let us not grumble that God hasn't given us enough time. He has. It is up to us to use it carefully.

Even older children benefit from having a "lights out" time. They might read in their beds for half an hour or more, but at some point it is time to respect the body's requirement for restoration and healing. In insisting upon a reasonable bedtime, you can work towards, and enjoy, a very quiet evening for yourself and your husband.

Quality sleep is achieved through routine, but also through an inviting bed, a warm bath, a cozy book, prayer, and a loving atmosphere in the home. All screens ought to be turned off well before sleep, and the room as dark as your children will allow. Our family turns off the internet router at night to decrease Wi-Fi waves while sleeping. Do your children a favor and keep all gadgets, TV's, and other unnecessary electrical equipment out of the room to ensure a more restful sleep, allowing their bodies to recover from the difficulties of living in the world.

Doing this Evening PRACTICE is going to make your next day far more happy, as well-rested children are less grumpy and ill. Who doesn't want happier and healthier children?

In the Resources section in the back, find our family's favorite bedtime books, put together by our children.

LOOK

LOOK at your calendar. It is the same routine as the Morning PRACTICE, except now you are looking to see if you have any appointments first thing in the next morning to be aware of, or plans for the coming day which need preparation. Are you taking your children out tomorrow? Do they have clean clothes ready?

PLAN

In the same way, decide what breakfast is going to be. Do you need to soak oats, count eggs, make sure there's milk? What about lunch? Are you eating at home, or do you need to consider something packable for the road? And what about supper? Do you need to take out meat to defrost, or do you need to soak beans overnight? Is there anything at all you can do this evening to make your meal preparation tomorrow more seamless? Deciding on meals now relieves a lot of stress the next day! You'll also feel better knowing your family is getting fed nutritious meals, and saving money besides.

CREATE

Because we were designed by a wise and generous Creator, we ourselves, in reflecting His image, are also creators. Perhaps a woman may not partake in a particular and well-known artistic endeavor such as painting with watercolors, knitting, or writing poetry, but that does not mean she is not creative. She may be able to arrange furniture so it is pleasing to the eye or make every meal a presentation. Or maybe she presents herself in a stylish way, or loves digging her hands into the mud with her children. But there is always something a woman is drawn to express in a creative way.

The PRACTICE is to spend some time in the evening expressing or playing with that creative side. I will try to answer to some objections.

I don't have enough time.
I believe it's close to a sin to say things like, "There isn't enough time in the day." Yes, yes there is. In fact, there is the perfect amount of hours in every single day because God created each day with the perfect amount of time. These daily hours are freely given to each and every person, every single day.

Many people forget their creative endeavors so easily played with when childhood was so free. Some painted, some wrote, some stacked rocks. Some pulled bicycles apart to fashion something new, and others drew fashion designs to pull together something old ("vintage" in today's language). Every child is attracted towards creativity in some sense, and needs good toys to encourage imagination.

But once children reach adulthood, the joys of creating seem to wane into the background, because "more important adult things" are louder. However, we see over and over again, instead of having paint time, we make time for screen time. Instead of tending to childhood hints of simple, creative pleasures, we do another load of laundry. We may think playing is childish, but the *time* is still there.

Even a short break for playtime is sweet. As FlyLady[22] says, "You can do anything for 15 minutes!" If you like to knit, do a few rows. If you like mixed media art, slap down some gesso. If you love to garden, plan out the next raised bed. And so forth. Little by little, 15 minutes by 15 minutes, you are building upon skills and getting projects done, but even those benefits are not the point. The point is to PLAY, to enjoy the process of the *thing* simply for the pleasure of *doing it,* no matter what the finished outcome is.

I don't have the materials.

This is merely a statement of fact, not a statement of hinderance. For example, if you would like to play around with watercolors, there are ample means by which to procure those watercolors, brushes, paper, and even classes should you desire to take them. Begin by making a list of what you would need to get started. I would advise you to limit the initial list to bare essentials. Why? Because you may decide once playing around, something else has caught your eye more, and you may end up changing directions, perhaps over and over and over again. And that's all right.

Also, you do not need to buy the most expensive materials available. However, I would encourage you to buy the best quality you can comfortably afford. Just because you *could* buy the children's watercolor set at the dollar store doesn't mean you ought to if you *could* buy the $15 set at the art store. Buying the best you can comfortably afford means you are likely to have more enjoyment and success. For example, sable watercolor brushes hold paint and water far longer than the synthetic brushes, which means a lot less dipping, dipping, dipping. Watercolors in tubes[23] from quality companies have real pigment in them, which means your pictures will be vibrant. Real watercolor paper[24] will be more forgiving than say, copy paper, which would soak up water and tear. It is not a waste of money to buy a few tools to PRACTICE and play with.

In the meantime, don't let your lack of materials hinder you! DO play with your children's watercolors while you wait for your own, better supplies. If you are wanting to try something out before purchasing, open your eyes to other possibilities: taking a class, renting, or borrowing.

I don't have room.

Well, I suppose it depends on what you're attempting to do. Dressage will take an entire arena with a horse, barn, and equipment. Perhaps it is not attainable where you currently are, but that doesn't make it impossible. It becomes a question to ponder, a problem to solve, *"Where* could I...?"

For creative endeavors at home, carving out room is simply a problem to be solved. Most of us are living in houses with more room than the majority of people on the planet have, so it may be simply a matter of decluttering and making room for new endeavors. If you have two living rooms, for example, but rarely use one, why not turn the unused place into a studio you would enjoy nearly every day? After all, unused floor space is part of the mortgage or rent you're paying, too!

For a long time, my craft table was our family meal table. All of my quilts were planned, cut and sewn after the last meal of the day. All of my family scrapbooks were organized, arranged, and decorated there in the evenings. Same for most of my blog posts, letters, and other paper crafts. Yes, it meant getting organized with storage bins between my creative times. But little by little, evening by evening, the quilts got finished, and so did the other projects.

When my husband, Tom, and I were in an apartment with two little children, part of a closet became an "office". When we were in our little cabin, we set up our podcast studio in a corner of the attic. For handwork such as spindle spinning, stitching, knitting and crochet, I used pretty baskets to keep fiber and yarn stored out of sight between sessions, and still do so today. My art supplies (of all sorts) continue to be organized into stacked, vintage leather suitcases.

There are many ways to make a place for your creativity to shine!

It will make a mess.
Yup. Not only in the doing of the *thing*, but also in the learning process. A delicious, fun, and exciting mess! Some people thrive on seeing all of the stuff out in the open for inspiration, and others want

everything put away and cleaned up. However way you find peace in your surroundings, accept there will be paint splotches and stray threads along the way. It is proof there is LIFE going on in the house, and YOU are part of that life.

I should be doing something else.

Maybe, but maybe not. Perhaps it is time to consider why you think so. Is it because a creative endeavor feels unnecessary? Or is because your housework was neglected until evening? In the former case, I would argue creative expression is absolutely necessary; it reflects God's character, is good for your mental health, and brings your beauty into the world. In the latter case, I would allow guilt to spur you to find a solution, yes, even a *creative* solution to getting your priorities accomplished.

Even if your day's work is undone, there needs to be a stopping point, to rest and to recoup. No matter how organized your chore lists are, no matter how perfectly run the day is, you will still have things in your inbox to deal with. Areas will still need cleaning. Emails will still need answering. Laundry will still need dealing with, somehow, and I bet there will still be a pile of homeschooling stuff that needs looking at. Our work will never be DONE until Jesus calls us home, so give yourself a stopping point in the evening to allow you to refresh your spirit in a creative, non- "necessary" way.

I don't know how to do it.

Welcome to the fun! We are living in a time where we can get instruction on ANYTHING right from our very own private computers via the Internet, and most of us still have the option to visit a library or two and come home with a pile of books. You can learn to knit socks through You Tube, or find drawing lessons through Pinterest. You can purchase entire downloadable classes, and some of these classes even involve direct participation with the instructor. I taught myself how to weave on a loom with a book, and asked (and ask) questions as needed through social media and local store connections.

When you are in the right season, you may have other options, such as taking a class in person. When I had littles at home, I took my first quilting class in the evening when Daddy was home. The funny thing was once I got there, I discovered I was supposed to bring a sewing machine. I had zero idea how to use

PRACTICES

one, and didn't own one either, but the instructors were so supportive and friendly. They not only allowed me to borrow a machine, they took time to teach me how to use it and how to make a quilt, besides. I've taken other classes, too, such as calligraphy, natural dyeing, botanical watercolors, beading, basketry, writing, using colored pencils, spinning (yarn), and more.

When you can get away for longer, even more options open up. I've taken several away-from-home art classes (you can read about one such trip in my book, *Present*).[25] In this manner, I've taken all sorts of classes: art journaling, watercoloring, encaustic painting, mixed media, leather bookmaking, herbal preparations, monoprinting, and more. Plus the delight of having time away to refresh with a friend is a wonderful blessing.

There is no end to what you can learn! If you don't have an idea of what you would enjoy, simply observe the kind of creative work your eye is naturally drawn to, and begin there. As an added benefit, your children see your continued curiosity and eagerness to learn, instilling in them a beautiful model that will serve them for a lifetime. Plus, they get to try the stuff you do!

I can't get it right.

You'll have to define "right". Do you mean not making mistakes? Consider how many times you fell down while learning to walk (17.4 times per hour according to a 2012 *Psychological Science* study). Did you stop getting up? Consider other areas you are more seasoned in, as well, such as cooking or teaching or even being a good friend. These were all areas you grew in over time. Did you not make mistakes along the way? Do you not STILL make mistakes?

Mistakes are not problems when you are taking pleasure in the task at hand. They are only problems when you have an unrealistic expectation of some level of perfection. We rejoice when we make mistakes, because as difficult/frustrating/hairpulling as it may be at the time (I've cut many wayward warps off my loom after many hours of threading), these mistakes become stepping stones to doing even better the next time.

Remember: the point is the pleasure and relaxation of the *doing*. The product is simply a beautiful bonus.

I'm too distracted.
Maybe. We do need to look at our time with sobriety and consider how we might better redeem the short, vapor-like time we have. Keep reading. We will get to how to incorporate the PRACTICES you desire, and in doing so, you may find your distractibility melting away.

Ultimately, in order to overcome hinderances to PRACTICES we desire to incorporate into our lives, we need to replace statements with "I can't..." or "I don't..." with the question, "How can I...?"

READ

I love to read before I go to sleep. I usually have a stack of books by my bedside, and they vary in topics. Most of the time, I choose nonfiction as I am trying to learn something new or discover something different – home design, health and wellness, creative inspiration, Christian living, and how-to books, all find a place in my reading time. Devotionals are very good at times, as are biographies and topics seemingly over my head such as the stock market. Believe it or not, business books are super helpful for the homefront, too: how to organize time, get things done, and not lose your mind in the process.

Rarely do I choose fiction, but there are seasons when I love it. Last summer I chose twelve books garnered from lists and reviews, and plowed through them. It was delightful and pure entertainment, totally getting lost in a good story, and, enjoying super fine writing, so satisfying and perhaps evoking a touch of writer-envy ("Oh, to put such a beautiful sentence together!"). I find what bothers me most about modern fiction is the increasing use of coarse language, or worldviews so anti-God I can't stand it. And, remember, this is supposed to be an Evening PRACTICE for me to *relax*. Often enough I am sent back to my nonfiction reading.

You can find ideas for books in many places: Amazon, Goodreads, or recommendations from bloggers and people you respect. The library is a great place to visit as you may end up in sections that initially sound boring, but find a real gem. Your local and independent bookstore is a terrific place to browse as well, and most owners are pleased to offer suggestions. If you find a good book there, please show your gratitude by purchasing it from them so they will stay in business.

You'll find a selection of books I've recently enjoyed in the Resources. I hope you'll find something new and interesting.

CONNECT

You need to connect with your spouse on a daily basis, physically, emotionally, and mentally.

Physically, we are not to abstain from one another unless we are in a time of fasting and prayer (1 Corinthians 7:5). I don't think this means we need to truly unite every single day, but there needs to be at least be physical touch of some sort. My husband loves his shoulders rubbed. I like his smooches. Holding hands and walking together, a loving stroke on the face, even a hug before someone heads out the door...all are important to communicate love.

Emotionally, our spouse needs to know we are trustworthy and are able to listen. There is so much to share with our spouses, from our wins of the day to our ongoing frustrations, from worries over deadlines to enthusiasm over the children's successes. Secrets are poison unless you're planning a surprise party. We know even secret sins will be found out, so remain open and honest with temptations and trials. Your spouse ought to be, second to Jesus, your very best friend.

Mentally, we need to challenge and encourage one another to grow in the faith and to strengthen our walks with the Lord. Sometimes it's good to simply listen to the troubles of the day, and other times it is good to mentally engage one another and come up with solutions to problems or to set and implement goals. From money issues to child raising to a whole host of other issues married couples deal with, there is no shortage of opportunity to encourage your spouse. Both of you are smart and resourceful, and together you can figure out what the next steps ought to be – even if it involves Biblical counseling.[26]

PRACTICES

The following are some thoughts regarding special challenges to CONNECTing:

My spouse is an unbeliever.

You are not alone. Many people marry unequally yoked and come to a terrible struggle. Others may have been equally yoked as unbelievers, but upon repentance thereby become strangers. 1 Peter 3 speaks to this issue, exhorting believers to steadfastly trust in God. Perhaps the unbelieving spouse will ultimately be won. Regardless of your spouse's salvation, love and respect is commanded by God, and it is our obedience and love of Christ that equips and enables us to do so. Furthermore, take heart; it is not our job to convert anyone. It is to share the gospel, and to let God work in the heart. Finally, remember Christ died for *sinners,* and it is our privilege to serve as He served, washing dirty feet.

My spouse is abusive.

If your spouse is abusing you, that is an issue for the law, which God has ordained to take care of criminals. I urge you to seek help immediately through your local church and local law enforcement. Because God is sovereign, He can be trusted with your spouse's future, even if that means jail, and your future as well. There is *never* an excuse for domestic violence, and it is NOT YOUR FAULT.

I don't have a spouse.
Blessed are you, then, to be able to focus on the things of the Lord more! During this time, you can be praying for whatever needs you have. Do you desire a spouse? Are you widowed? Separated or divorced? Depending on your situation, you may need to pray for contentment in being alone while waiting, or for your wayward spouse to repent and/or seek reconciliation. You may need to go through Biblical counseling[25] over your unique challenge, need, or trial.

My spouse is away a lot.
Business trips and military tours of duty are real challenges, especially because temptations to partake in pornography or adultery are stronger in these times. I urge you to study the scriptures in how to battle and win over temptations, and to do what you can to maintain CONNECTion with your spouse: praying for him, writing to him, FaceTime or email, etc.

Even if you have special challenges in the romance department, you can make an effort to CONNECT with people in some way on a regular basis. Calling and hearing another person's voice (hopefully not while multitasking on screens), or sitting down to write a letter or a postcard to an old friend are other good ways to CONNECT with someone. Don't fall into the traps of thinking typed texts and social media updates are enough; most of the time we think those are valid ways of CONNECTing, but we often type rather than talk due to avoidance, laziness, or self-centeredness. We have to examine our hearts if we are failing to CONNECT. CONNECTing is so important a PRACTICE.

PRAY

Nevertheless we made our prayer unto our God...
– Nehemiah 4:9

Maybe it seems strange prayer is listed as a PRACTICE. In one sense, we ought to be praying unceasingly, always in the spirit, throughout our day. This is true. However, it seems a bit too much like multitasking, something akin to listening to music while doing the dishes, or speaking to a friend while folding the laundry. Not bad things whatsoever, but still an attention divided. I'm not sure our attention to the Creator of the universe ought to be so regularly divided.

There is never enough time in the day or words in our language to give God all of the glory He is due, but we must give Him preference at some portion of our day. The psalmist speaks of meeting with Him both at the start and at the finish:

> *My voice shalt thou hear in the morning, O LORD; in the morning will I direct my prayer unto thee, and will look up.*
> – Psalms 5:3
>
> *Let my prayer be set forth before thee as incense; and the lifting up of my hands as the evening sacrifice.*
> – Psalms 141:2

Countless Christian books have been written on the importance of prayer, and many have been helpful to me. The most recent one I've come across

PRACTICES

is *A Praying Life*.[27] It is written to the Christians of today: rushed, distracted, and too independent for their own good. It's an easy read, highly encouraging, and gives practical, real-life help from a real-life man who struggles with prayer like you and me. I didn't mind his stories, because in many ways, they were mine too.

If you're looking for more depth in the study of prayer, you may like *Prayer*[28] by O. Hallesby. This book helped me tremendously when I was newly saved and still is one of my favorites today.

I urge you to not neglect the PRACTICES of prayer and of reading the Bible. Let God speak to you through His Word. And let Him hear you through your quiet, faithful, undistracted prayers.

CHAPTER FOUR

Implement

...Pass the time of your sojourning here in fear...that your faith and hope might be in God.
– 1 Peter 1:17, 21

Ideas are useless unless used. The proof of their value is in their implementation.
– Theodore Levitt

PERHAPS AT THIS POINT you are feeling inspired and have already bought blank journals, books to read, and a sleep mask. Or maybe you're feeling overwhelmed, because you want to do them ALL but don't know how to start. Wherever you are in this process, remember the point is *not* to get busier and sleep less, but to hone in on those

PRACTICES enabling to you be more in touch with your God, more present with your family, and happier with the ebb and flow of your days.

KEEP THE MAIN THING THE MAIN THING

For the Christian, absolutely two main PRACTICES ought to be reading the Bible, and spending time in prayer. As a friend recently relayed to me, you don't need to "find yourself" by doing anything else, because you are *found* in Christ. Commit now to not allow a day to pass without spending set-apart time with God. He is your rest. Again, let us not neglect so great a salvation.

SEASONS

There are times in your life when you will have greater stretches of time and resources than others.

You may be in a season with a newborn and toddlers, exhausted. You may be in transition, with children either growing up and leaving home, or newly married, or about to embark on caring for an elderly parent. Every season has its blooming and

PRACTICES

waning, and yours is no different. Your PRACTICES will change and evolve as your circumstances do; implement wisely and adjust as needed.

You also may find one PRACTICE simply doesn't fit because it doesn't help in the way you had hoped. If this is the case, I'd ask you to consider:

- What about that particular PRACTICE appealed to you to begin with? Can you tweak it?

- Did you give it a good go for a decent run, of, say, 60 days?

- Is the reason you're uncomfortable with it because it's bringing up problems you've been putting off thinking about?

- Is what you were hoping this PRACTICE would do for you a reasonable hope?

- Was your goal for this PRACTICE measurable in any way? For example, if you aren't reading "enough", maybe you need to apply a measure, such as "read 15 minutes".

Just because something is difficult doesn't mean it's not your season, personalty, or talent. Give yourself the opportunity through persistence to overcome the initial difficulties or disappointments. Remember what drew you to the idea of PRACTICES, and let it guide you through any changes you may need to make.

CHRISTIAN LIBERTY

None of this is mandatory. You will not lose your salvation if you don't make your bed or eat a nourishing breakfast. Furthermore, live a life of making small changes to see progress, not perfection. Keep tweaking your PRACTICES until you are at a place of contentment and peace through your day, knowing that only being with Jesus in heaven will give you full satisfaction. Don't give up your daily walk if you miss a few days; there's no judgment in beginning again, and there is absolutely no pressure to maintain any PRACTICE at all. Remember that these are tools to help you, not tasks to push you. You always have liberty to start, stop, change, and try something different. That being said, I hope you'll give maintaining PRACTICES a good go. The 60 Day Calendar is offered here to as a tool to help in that endeavor.

60 DAY CALENDAR

In the Resources, you'll find a 60 day calendar to help you decide upon, and mark your progress in, developing habitual and helpful PRACTICES. I've divided the calendar into three sets of twenty as a reasonable measure to see how you are progressing.

For the first twenty days, add whatever PRACTICE you like. If you struggle with reading the Bible and prayer, then stay there. If you are already practicing those, add another PRACTICE to the morning and maybe one to the evening. You don't have to do both. You can concentrate only on your morning, for example.

Reassess after the first twenty days. If the PRACTICES you are attempting to implement are feeling pretty good, then add more if you wish. If a

PRACTICE is not working for you at all, consider the questions I posed previously and decide if you need to make a change.

I would encourage you NOT to simply "try this-try that" without giving a particular PRACTICE a fair run. I believe 60 days to be fair. The point is not to try as many ideas as possible, but to find the pearls that will sustain you over a long time, perhaps a lifetime. Give those new PRACTICES a chance to settle in, to get to the other side of the initial discomfort of trying something new.

IN CLOSING

Remember WHY you wanted to make a change. We intuitively know and understand our lives are speeding along too fast, and daily we miss those important moments enriching our relationships. If there is any sort of angst or anxiety or rush, let it be for good reason and not simply because it's Monday, or Thursday, or Sunday.

PRACTICES take *practice*. Even when doing them consistently, your days still may be long, but they will be more peaceful and full of purpose, and you will

PRACTICES

get more things done without working harder than you need to. Full days, yes, but tremendously satisfying, even if those years are short. Soon you will discover which PRACTICES fuel your energy levels and which habits drain them. Such knowledge, with practical application, is powerful.

May you be blessed as you seek to cultivate a happier home, to God's glory.

RESOURCES

BY NOW YOU SEE your own unique PRACTICES will have their own unique requirements to fulfill them. The resources in this section are obviously not the only helps you may need, but they are starting points if you desire a gentle push.

Many books and resources have been shared throughout these pages – look into them one at a time, for whichever PRACTICE you are wanting to pursue on. If a particular resource isn't helpful, do not give up on your PRACTICE! Dig up your tenacity and use your stubborn streak to focus and find the help you need to succeed. You are not doing anything *new*, and you are not beyond *help*. If you're alive and breathing, you can renew your mind and create new habits.

KERI MAE LAMAR

PRACTICES

SOME GOOD READS

The only Book I *wholeheartedly* recommend is the Bible; it is the most important read of the day. My second recommendation would be any book on any topic of interest to you, including any previously referenced in this book. Third, below find several good books I have read and enjoyed enough to pass along for your consideration. These are not necessarily Christian books, so I cannot endorse everything within them, of course, but I have enjoyed them.

- *All the Light We Cannot See*
  by Anthony Doerr (historical fiction) –
  ahappyhomemedia.com/lightwecannotsee

- *The Nightingale*
  by Kristin Hannah (historical fiction) –
  ahappyhomemedia.com/nightingale

- *The Solace of Water*
  by Elizabeth Byler Younts
  (historical fiction) –
  ahappyhomemedia.com/solacewater

- *Deep Work*
  by Cal Newport
  (a business book with practical applications) –
  ahappyhomemedia.com/deepwork

- *Fearless Writing*
  by William Kenower
  (on the subject of, what else, writing) –
  ahappyhomemedia.com/fearlesswriting

- *The Hands-On Home: A Seasonal Guide to Cooking, Preserving & Natural Homekeeping*
  by Erica Strauss (I love this book for seasonal homemaking helps – like PRACTICES for the seasons) –
  ahappyhomemedia.com/handsonhome

Our Family Favorite Bedtime Books

- *The Sleep Ponies*
  by Gudrun Ongman –
  ahappyhomemedia.com/sleepponies

- *My Pony*
  by Susan Jeffers –
  ahappyhomemedia.com/mypony

PRACTICES

- *Five Little Monkeys Jumping on the Bed*
    by Eileen Christelow –
    ahappyhomemedia.com/fivelittlemonkeys

- *Pete the Cat*
    by James Dean –
    ahappyhomemedia.com/petethecat

- *Don't Let the Pigeon Drive the Bus!*
    by Mo Willems –
    ahappyhomemedia.com/pigeonbus

- *Fancy Nancy*
    by Jane O'Connor –
    ahappyhomemedia.com/fancynancy

- *Dinosaur Roar!*
    by Henrietta Stickland –
    ahappyhomemedia.com/dinosaurroar

- *Baby Beluga*
    by Raffi –
    ahappyhomemedia.com/babybeluga

- *Sing a Song*
  by June Melser –
  ahappyhomemedia.com/singasong

- *We're Going on a Bear Hunt*
  by Helen Oxenbury –
  ahappyhomemedia.com/bearhunt

- *The Bear Went Over the Mountain*
  by Rosemary Wells –
  ahappyhomemedia.com/bearovermountain

PRACTICES

JOURNAL PROMPTS

1) If I had time to relax, I would....

2) My inner critic says ____ But God says....

3) Ten things I own that touch my heart and why they do

4) I am 9 years old. I am....

5) What I would tell that 9 year old now is....

6) I remember the house on....

7) If money or time weren't an issue, I would....

8) These are the people I am most grateful for in my life....

9) My 10 biggest wishes are....

10) Looking at my wishes, 10 tiny steps could be....

11) I wish people knew I needed....

12) When I am an old woman, I will....

13) I feel pretty when....

14) A Bible verse I read, _____, made me think of....

15) I'm afraid of _____ but God says....

16) Favorite foods I truly enjoy

17) People I admire and why I do

18) Small things I can do to emulate the people I admire

19) I am happy when....

20) I feel vulnerable when....

21) What I most want to learn right now is....

22) Twenty tasks that I could do in just 15 minutes or less

23) If I had an hour to myself, I would....

PRACTICES

24) Ten small gifts to myself that I would enjoy

25) What my husband needs most from me is....

26) Write about each child, person, or pet you care for, and your hopes for each.

27) I love the smell of....

28) A list of small things I could do to freshen up my home

29) Jesus has been teaching me....

30) If I had more courage....

31) If I weren't so distracted by my screen time, I might....

32) If I really believed time was short, I would....

33) What makes me angry is....

34) If I had a free hour in town, I would....

35) I am most worried about _____ but God says....

36) Fifteen questions I am curious about

37) The projects I would most like to do include....

38) Write out the Bible verses you know you need most to memorize.

39) I would like to be known as....

40) If it didn't sound crazy, I would....

41) The people in my life need....

42) A list of all of the places I have lived

43) How can I get the time/classes/money I need to meet my goals?

44) My strengths include....

45) Ten things I'd like to read or learn more about

PRACTICES

46) My family wishes I would....

47) Five people I could send a postcard or a snail mail letter to

48) The book I'm reading right now....

49) At the end of the day, I want to feel....

50) A list of my energizers and a list of my energy-drainers

51) Ways my family can spend more quality time together include....

52) An ad for the mentor I always wanted, and how I as a mentor in training could grow into that picture

53) My testimony of God's grace in the last week....

54) If I could go back to school, I would....

55) The one thing I hope to accomplish today is....

56) Ways I could show my husband how much I respect and love him

57) Write out prayers for the day.

58) I feel most secure when....

59) I laugh when....

60) When I finish this notebook, I am going to....

PRACTICES

OTHER MAMA PRACTICES

Below, find beautiful and unique PRACTICES from a multitude of women of all ages. Some of these women are single (either unmarried, divorced, or widowed), and some are married, with or without children (from babyhood to adulthood). All have found keeping PRACTICES helpful, and they have graciously shared some of their own PRACTICES with you. Be encouraged!

Rebecca
I keep a prayer list inside my bathroom cabinet and pray while I brush my teeth. Simultaneously I do a 2 min wall sit (strengthen core). I start my day with the Bible, and did when I had kids too. We studied together before we started any other school. It set the tone.

Paige
Morning

- Read my Bible, as well as a devotion of some sort (recommended reading: *The*

Valley of Vision,[29] by Arthur Bennett or *Let Me Be a Woman*,[30] by Elisabeth Elliot).

- Pray

- Step outside into the sunshine, just for a minute.

- Put on makeup. I don't wear a lot, so this doesn't take long at all. It makes me feel put together.

Evening

- Comfy and fashionable p.j.s are nice. "Fashionable" is up to you. I like a t-shirt and lounge pants.

- I started a gratitude journal this year. (Almost) every night I jot down a list of 5 things I'm grateful for.

- A warm milk drink

- Reading a bit before bed

- Writing to my pen-pals

PRACTICES

Michele

In the evening, as part of the "cleaning the kitchen from dinner" routine, the table is set for breakfast. I also prep for breakfast. If we're having pancakes, dry ingredients are mixed together, ready to be added to the wet ingredients, while the bowl for the wet ingredients and the whisk are ready on the counter. If oatmeal, I'll place the pan on the stove, add the water, and salt, to be boiled and cover with a lid while placing the stack of bowls nearby. Besides being part way ready, these things will provide visual clues as to what needs to be done next as I enter the kitchen with many other things already on my mind the next morning. Consideration is also made for what we'll be having for dinner the following evening. I can defrost meat if needed. Or if beans need to soak, I can either start the process or set the beans on the counter to remind myself to start them in the morning.

Kelly

I have animals that constantly need care. Unless we are away on vacation or I am sick in bed, I have to go outside, first thing every morning and last thing every night. When the responsibilities of animal husbandry feels like a burden, I try to remember all the benefits. Physically getting out of my man-made environment and entering into God's-made environment has a wonderful way of recentering, relaxing and restoring my soul. I almost always enjoy a new perspective just from stepping out the door. Although we've lived in the same place for 36 years, each day is full of beauty to be discovered. Feeling the weather change with the seasons, listening to the birds singing and the wind blowing, breathing fresh air, watching the changes in the sky high overhead, and interacting with critters who trust you and enjoy your company, are some of life's most simple and yet profound blessings.

Claire

Each morning and evening I enjoy taking care of the animals. It forces me to take a quiet moment to watch the sunset, smell the flowers, gaze at the stars, and reflect on the day. I like to pray each night before I fall asleep. Taking all my worries and cares to Jesus helps me to be at peace. Each morning I make a list of "things to do today" in my planner. It helps me to remember the important things that need to be completed that day.

PRACTICES

Molly

One thing that really helps me in the morning, as I have a nursing baby, is to have my other children make breakfast. I can focus on getting myself and Baby ready for the day in a calm fashion. And my children learn the terrific skill of making food for the family. We then all eat and have a Bible study together.

> *Return, O my soul, to your rest; for the LORD has dealt bountifully with you.*
> *– Psalms 116:7*

Abby

Evening

- Dishwasher is loaded and started

- Downstairs is relatively picked up/clean

- Early evening gather all the dirty clothes from around the house (minus my two older boys-they do their own laundry) and start a load, moving it before I go to sleep. If I get this done early enough, it's dry before I go to sleep and I go ahead and sort it out into people's bins to be put away in the morning (by them).

- Make sure I have written down what we are having for breakfast/lunch/dinner for the next day and pull anything necessary from the freezer.

- If I'm really on top of things I will go ahead and pull out my morning homeschool read-alouds, bible memory box, etc. and set those on the kitchen table.

- I don't always do this but it really does help my mornings if in the evenings I take a shower and lay out my clothes for the next day.

- Plug my phone into the charger in the kitchen and place it in the basket. I do not bring it upstairs with me to my bedroom.

- One of my most helpful things is to plan out my next day. I have a small chalkboard that has a little stand (like a picture frame

PRACTICES

that you can set on a table) that I bought at Hobby Lobby. I hate the feel and sound of chalk but they make amazing white chalk markers that are nice and smooth. So along with the help of my day planner/calendar, I write out what's coming up the next day. This is where I write what we will be eating, a schedule of appointments if any coming up and anything I especially need to get accomplished during the next day. It's not where I write down my master schedule or daily routine – that's just already in place. It's the extra stuff.

- It's my desire to end the day with kneeling prayer, pouring out my heart to God.

As you can see my evenings are the key to success for the following morning/day. My morning routine flows from how diligent I was in my evening routine.

Morning
- I typically wake up and my thoughts turn into prayers to God for the day and whatever else is on my heart. For the first

30 minutes or so of the day while I'm still upstairs getting ready I usually have a conversation going with God.

- Drink a large glass of water (I always bring a large glass of water up to my room with me at night so I can take my medicine in the morning)

- I wish my time in the Word was more set in stone in my routine but it tends to find it's place floating – sometimes in the evening if I'm not too terribly sleepy, sometimes in the morning and sometimes in the early afternoon.

- Sometimes I shower in the morning, sometimes in the evening. After getting dressed I go downstairs and make sure the boys are moving on their chores.

- Once I'm downstairs I will spend 3-4 minutes typically just checking in with my phone – email, texts, messages from my best friend who is in a different time zone as a missionary in Romania. She has often

PRACTICES

messaged me by the time I wake up since that is her afternoon :) Once I've read everything and responded to anything urgent, my phone goes back in the basket.

And now the day begins!

Diane

- Read *Morning and Evening*[31] by Charles Spurgeon.

- Pray the Acts model after the Spurgeon reading. (Google it for more explanation).

    A - adoration
    C - confession
    T - thanksgiving
    S - supplication

- Read through the Bible once every year.

- Memorize and pray the 23rd Psalm before you go to sleep.

- DAILY, I carry around with me the thought that I am Christ's bride. It rescues me from many a depression, sickness and/or emotional meltdown. It is a high calling and an intimate reality.

In reflection this list should not imprison us, but free us. It is not another mandate but a strategy for glorifying our Lord and grounding us in first things.

There is not one person who, at the end of their life said, "why didn't I dust more"! Enjoy your family and Praise your Lord!

Katharine
A couple things from me:
- Empty and stock the diaper bag when I get home from using it instead of when I'm trying to leave the house AND put it back into the car or have it near the front door

- Set out kids clothes if I want them to wear something specific instead of whatever they grab out of their closets or just accept what my 3 and 4 year olds pick out.

- Have a plan for breakfast

PRACTICES

Crystal

To protect my morning quiet time from mental interruptions, aka – what are we doing for breakfast, I try to plan ahead the night before. Whether that requires pulling meat out of the freezer or taking a peek into the leftovers, or specifically making more pork chops for dinner to have sliced meat to warm up in the morning with veggies (good before running off to morning Bible Study Fellowship), then I am mentally prepared and know what time prerequisite is needed.

In my season of life I cannot "let everyone fend for themselves" for the most important meal of the day. Neither can I afford the distractions to my most important meal of the day – God's Word.

Mary

As a single mom of two, I always had to work outside the home. With a 18 month old and a newborn evening consisted of getting bags ready for the next day and spending as much time with them that I could. Then doing any household chores that needed to be done. I did not take much time for God or myself except for church on Sunday. In retrospect, I see that if I had given God more of my time and consideration, stress and sometimes chaos would have been reduced.

As the children grew they of course were part of the routine. On Sunday after church we would sit down and plan the weekly meals and determine what activities were on the calendar for the week.

Mornings consisted of getting breakfast, dressed, and off to the sitter and me to work. Then on my way to work I saw God's glory in the scenery – mountains, trees, clouds, and the feeling of His goodness. I talked to Him while driving to work. What a peaceful time. Evenings were spent with dinner, homework (for the children and myself since I was also in college), reviewing commitments for the next day, getting clothes ready for all of us, then falling into bed reviewing my prayer list and praying before falling asleep.

As I reflect, I certainly didn't put an emphasis on studying His word, but always knew of His presence and wonder.

PRACTICES

Belinda

What helps me most in the morning is to get up before the house awakens and have quiet time with the Lord and myself; how I wish I did it more often. But I do wake up and give thanks before arising (I have heard it called "giving him your waking thoughts"). Planning from the day before helps, and then prioritizing the 1-2 things that MUST happen (I have heard this called the "power hour").

The nighttime routine? Writing at least one thing that I am thankful for on the gratitude page of my bullet journal. I DO NOT watch news at night. Also, most nights, I am in bed early enough to get good rest.

Sue

I get up before anyone else to have a cuppa, sip while looking outside, meditating, praying for our friends and family. I like to consider what God's teaching me in the moment. As He speaks through something as simple as a flower, a bee, a blade of grass or the trees waving in the breeze...it gives me a moment to settle into a new day. I'll think about what needs to be accomplished, and try to balance those thoughts with our main purpose – to glorify God in all that we do and say.

During the September-May, I do my Bible Study Fellowship daily studies in the mornings.

Evenings are when my husband and I read aloud in bed together from an inspiring biography of a Christian, then we listen to a themed "Nightsounds" program to go to sleep. When I awaken in the night, I have some soft "Sleep Phones" that I use to listen to Bible readings on Bible Gateway, or sometimes take in a podcast I've been wanting to hear but have not had the opportunity to listen to.

That's about it for morning and evening rituals.

It's like coming to two altars each day – one in the morning, and one in the evening. I look forward to those moments.

Cathy
I wish I had Morning Practices when my kids were home- most days felt like sheer survival. One thing I did do was always write out the next days focus points (pray, do laundry, make menu, etc) so that I

got up with purpose, it also helped me to feel like I actually accomplished something when I was able to cross them off my list. If I forgot to do that, days seem to hit me and roll over me like a wave.

Abby Jo
I like to simply make a list every night of my plans for the next day; it helps me stay on track. Example; oats and yogurt for breakfast, girls clean bathroom, start school by 9 am, go to the store and pick up dairy, and veg. Lunch? Dinner Roast chicken, mashed potatoes and peas. Test one of the kids on spelling and make sure I take a walk! I hope this helps :)

KERI MAE LAMAR

PRACTICES

60 DAY CALENDAR

The 60 day PRACTICES Calendar is simply another tool that may help you overcome resistance and allow you the feedback you need to persevere.

Download your own copy:[32]
AHappyHomeMedia.com/Practices60DayCalendar

I personally find crossing off lists, or days, very motivating and satisfying. If that's not you, you don't need to use this calendar. But if you're not making progress on your goals or are unhappy with how your days flow, then using this calendar perhaps needs to become "you". Try it; you might like it.

Sixty days seem more likely to cultivate a habit that sticks, so you'll see days numbered 1-60. I've divided those into three sets of twenty, to allow for tweaks as needed.

To begin, start with Set 1. List up to three Morning PRACTICES, and three Evening PRACTICES. Keep in mind that if you are starting from scratch, that is a lot! If there are already PRACTICES you are comfortable doing, you don't need to add them here. Simply add the PRACTICE you feel will best help you meet and close your days.

After adding those PRACTICES, jot down three short notes about WHY each particular PRACTICE will help you. For example:

- PRACTICE "a" for the morning: *journaling*

PRACTICES

- Why it would help me: *play with poetry, clears my mind, reminds me of goals*

The example above would remind me, when I got to day 8 or 17, for example, WHY I added *journaling* as a PRACTICE. I wanted to write more poetry (a creative endeavor). I wanted to get my busy thoughts out of my head. I wanted to remember the goals I had set and to think on paper what step should be next.

After going through the first set of 20 days, reassess. Do you feel good about the PRACTICES you've been implementing? If you're thinking of quitting a particular PRACTICE, have you given them a fair go, perhaps at least 80 percent of those first 20 days?

At this point, you can either rewrite your same PRACTICES (your reasons WHY may have changed), or add some new ones if you are already comfortable with your new habits.

All that being said, feel free to use this calendar any way you like! It is meant as a tool to help you, not as a master to enslave you. So pick a pretty color to fill in those boxes as you go, and do the hard work of getting to a better place in your life and home.

LINKS

Chapter 1: First Things First

1. *Moment* app – inthemoment.io

Chapter 2: Morning Practices

Awaken

2. My mattress – ahappyhomemedia.com/mymattress

3. Medication side effects – drugs.com

4. Insomnia and homeopathy – joettecalabrese.com/blog/insomnia-homeopathy

5. Biblical counseling – biblicalcounseling.com

Study

6. *Webster's 1828 Dictionary* – ahappyhomemedia.com/1828dictionary

7. King James Bible – kjvbible.net

8   Listen to the Bible – bible.is/apps

9   Bible study – precept.org

10 Scripture memory – scripturememory.com

Write

11 Jet Pens – jetpens.com

12 My favorite Jet Pen – ahappyhomemedia.com/myjetpen

Bathe

13 Vitabath – ahappyhomemedia.com/safebath

Nourish

14 Real extra virgin olive oil – ahappyhomemedia.com/realoliveoil

15 *The Nourished Metabolism* by Elizabeth Walling– ahappyhomemedia.com/nourishedmetabolism

PRACTICES

16 Vitaclay pot – ahappyhomemedia.com/vitaclay

Move

17 MutuSystem – ahappyhomemedia.com/mutu

Learn

18 Albert Mohler's *The Briefing* podcast – albertmohler.com/the-briefing

Plan

19 How pork affects your blood – ahappyhomemedia.com/porkblood

Chapter 3: Evening Practices

Clear the Sink

20 Mrs20. Meyer's Dish Soap (pine scent) – ahappyhomemedia.com/mydishsoap

21 Zum Clean (sea salt) – ahappyhomemedia.com/mycleaner

Create

22 FlyLady – flylady.net

23 Watercolors I like, in a sample sheet to play with, until you decide if it's for you or not – ahappyhomemedia.com/watercolorsamplesheet

24 Paper. I'm not picky about watercolor paper brands (yet, I guess); here is one I've used before and enjoyed. I like to cut the paper down to smaller sizes – ahappyhomemedia.com/watercolorpaper

25 My book, *Present* – ahappyhomemedia.com/present

26 Biblical counseling – biblicalcounseling.com

Pray

27 *A Praying Life* by Paul Miller – ahappyhomemedia.com/aprayinglife

28 *Prayer* by O. Hallesby – ahappyhomemedia.com/prayerthebook

PRACTICES

Resources

Other Mama Practices

    29 *The Valley of Vision*
by Arthur Bennett –
ahappyhomemedia.com/valleyofvision

    30 *Let Me Be a Woman*
by Elizabeth Elliot –
ahappyhomemedia.com/letmebeawoman

    31 *Morning and Evening*
by Charles Spurgeon –
ahappyhomemedia.com/
morningandevening

60 Day Calendar

    32 Download your own *60 Day Calendar* –
ahappyhomemedia.com/
practices60daycalendar

Next Steps

    33 A Happy Home Media's email list signup –
ahappyhomemedia.com/emailsignup

    34 Subscribe to *A Happy Home Podcast* –
ahappyhomemedia.com/itunessubscribe

35 Get my book, *Present* –
    ahappyhomemedia.com/buypresent

36 Review my book, *Present*, on Amazon –
    ahappyhomemedia.com/reviewpresent

37 Review *Practices* on Amazon –
    ahappyhomemedia.com/reviewpractices

38 Leave a podcast review on iTunes –
    ahappyhomemedia.com/itunesreview

39 Join us on Patreon –
    ahappyhomemedia.com/patreon

PRACTICES

NEXT STEPS

Thank you for reading this book. I pray you have found it pleasurable, hopeful, and helpful. Tom and I appreciate our readers and listeners, and enjoy our Happy Home community. Would you like to join us?

- ☐ Sign up on A Happy Home Media's email list[33] to get first notice of new blogs, podcasts, books, and programs.

- ☐ Subscribe to *A Happy Home Podcast*.[34]

- ☐ If you're struggling with focus, purchase my book, *Present,* from Amazon.[35]

- ☐ If you've read *Present*, please leave me a review on Amazon![36]

- ☐ Leave a review for PRACTICES on Amazon.[37]

- ☐ Leave a podcast review on iTunes.[38]

- ☐ Join us on Patreon![39] You'll love seeing our behind-the-scenes antics, and we'll love interacting with you as a part of our Happy Home community.

My Practices

MORNING

KERI MAE LAMAR

PRACTICES

EVENING

KERI MAE LAMAR

PRACTICES

SEASONAL

OTHER BOOKS BY KERI MAE

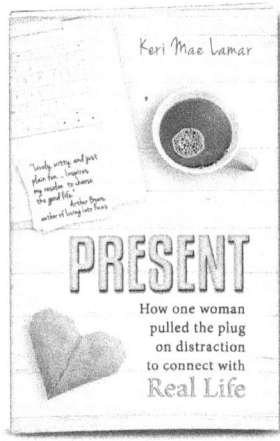

PRESENT: How one woman pulled the plug on distraction to connect with Real Life

Available at Amazon.com and other online book sellers in paperback, digital, and audio formats.

Learn more at AHappyHomeMedia.com/Present

*Happy is that people, that is in such a case:
yea, happy is that people, whose God is the Lord.*

– Psalm 144:15

www.ingramcontent.com/pod-product-compliance
Lightning Source LLC
Chambersburg PA
CBHW071119160426
43196CB00013B/2633